A YOUNG GIRL READING
Jean-Honoré Fragonard
National Gallery of Art, Washington, D.C.
Gift of Mrs. Mellon Bruce
in memory of her father, Andrew W. Mellon

E N G L A N D
THE FOUR SEASONS

Photographs by Michael Busselle
Commentary by Ronald Blythe

PAVILION

This edition published in Great Britain in 2000 by
PAVILION BOOKS LIMITED
London House, Great Eastern Wharf
Parkgate Road, London SW11 4NQ

Text © Ronald Blythe 1993, 2000
Photography © Michael Busselle 1993, 2000

The moral right of the author and illustrator
has been asserted

Designed by Andrew Barron & Collis Clements Associates

A CIP catalogue record for this book is available
from the British Library.

ISBN 1 86205 308 1

Set in New Baskerville
Printed in Singapore by Kyodo Printing Company

2 4 6 8 10 9 7 5 3 1

Illustrated on page one:
The Aysgarth Fall in Wensleydale, North Yorkshire.
Illustrated on page two:
Summer flowers above the Darent valley in Kent.
Illustrated on page three:
Farndale in the North York Moors.

This book can be ordered direct from the publisher.
Please contact the Marketing Department.
But try your bookshop first.

CONTENTS

THE LAND displays itself in four distinctive climates year after year. There are aberrations – snow in summer, an autumn gale which can blow away a million trees, an occasional arctic cold – but on the whole the seasons succeed each other with the temperatures, colours and moods which the people of these islands have long come to expect of them. England itself has come to expect a little less winter than Scotland, not as much rain as Wales and Ireland, but its seasonal changes are as influential as ever they were. They have helped to make us what we are. With their four defined bouts of weather and degrees of light, they provide a near-obsessional interest and fascination, as well as the most legitimate subject for our small talk. The spring continues to be less enchanting than we remembered, the summer goes on being glorious by fits and starts, the autumn pursues winter, catching up with its bitterness at last, and the winter is usually blamed for not being wintry enough. And so the English year goes round, dragging ourselves as well as the rest of nature with it, marking our lives and doing far more than politics to shape our national characteristics, did we but know it.

We have never been alone in the fervour of our season watching, although we rather like to think it. Two thousand years ago in China the poet Huai-nan Tzu decided that the human race, plus all living creatures, were created out of the scraps which were left over when the seasons themselves were invented. And it was a Sioux philosopher who gave one of the best descriptions of that yearly movement which carries us all along:

> Even the seasons form a great circle in their changing, and always come
> back again to where they were. The life of a man is a circle from
> childhood to childhood, and so it is in everything where power moves.
> Our tepees were round like the nests of birds, and these were always set
> in a circle, the nation's hoop.

The seasons, of course, are those segments of annual time caused by the earth's ever-altering position in relation to the sun. As it moves from equinox to solstice, and then from solstice to equinox, lengthening and shortening the light, increasing and decreasing warmth, the sun puts the landscape through its yearly paces. Religion kept step and there was never a time, except perhaps now, when the natural order – of the crops especially – and the sacred order were not in tandem. It is this duality which still forms the basis of the idealized view of the English countryside. For that is not one of wild moors and mountains, but of an old village with its architecture half sunk in trees and farmlands, with its river and flowers and May skies, or equally half sunk in snow. If it was the church calendar which tied our ancestors so providentially (and so remorselessly) to the seasons, for us it is now the shocking discovery that they could be finite. Nobody ever thought this before. 'While the earth remaineth, seedtime and harvest, and cold and heat, and summer and winter, and day and night shall not cease', was the ancient seasonal assurance. Now we are far from sure. Less devastating is the fact that fruits no longer have to be within season. Nobody could have imagined this before. It is a blessing and yet not a blessing, for the flavour of strawberries, raspberries and peas can never be the same now that they can be eaten all the year round.

From Geoffrey Chaucer to Ted Hughes, English literature has a structure almost as seasonally based as English agriculture. It is our window on to six hundred years of landscape and a running statement of attitudes towards scenery, weather and earthly views generally. We can put it beside the Ordnance Survey maps and current travelogues to see the losses and gains. We can also see that those who walked out on an April day in 1392 or 1892 did so with pleasures and expectations which were much the same as ours. It was springtime. This positive reaction to the changing year was ultimately set out in all its detail in a not very good but best-selling poem, James Thomson's *The Seasons*. Thomson, a 26-year-old Border Scot, had received such glowing praise for a poem called *Winter* that he went on to narrate in copious detail the character of all the seasons. He also wrote *Rule, Britannia*. His once immensely popular *The Seasons* is only interesting now because it allows us to glimpse what the eighteenth century loved or loathed about the year. Summer with its 'pestilential heats' was half-dreaded, as was winter – Robert Burns's 'maniac winter'. But spring was blissful and autumn was for meditation. Many years later a Northamptonshire farm-boy, John Clare, read *The Seasons*, with astounding results. For it began the process which led him to write *The Shepherd's Calendar*, that brilliant and unrivalled account of what really happens in the English countryside as the year passes. He tells how this occurred:

> I think I was 13 years of age now, but trifling things are never punctually remembered . . . This summer I met with a fragment of Thomson's Seasons, a young man, by trade a weaver, much older than myself, then in the village, show'd it me. I knew nothing of blank verse, not rhyme either, otherwise than by the trash of Ballad Singers, but I still remember my sensations in reading the opening of Spring. I can't say the reason . . . I greedily read over all I could before I returned it, and resolved to possess one myself, the price of it being only 1s.6d. I

expressed my surprise at seeing such a fine poem so carelessly handled, most part of Winter being gone, but the owner only laugh'd at me . . .

A few days later John Clare tramped the eight miles to Stamford and bought *The Seasons* for a shilling. Worried to be seen reading a book on a work day, he hid behind Lord Exeter's park wall. On the way home he began to compose his first poem, *The Morning Walk*. In 1827, just a century or so after Thomson had so delighted the public, Clare published his rural masterpiece, *The Shepherd's Calendar*, which pleased nobody. The world had changed even if the seasons had not and, as the painter John Constable discovered, the English at that moment did not want the facts of country life as the climate presented them, month after month; it still wanted spring, summer, etc. seen as clichés and moralities. Eventually, Thomas Hardy would make his characters act out their existence in genuine and strongly-felt seasons, both in towns and villages, and most of all in the fields and meadows. The summer which Tess spends on the dairy farm is a masterly piece of seasonal writing in which Hardy is able to reveal the languor and sensuality which can invade the landscape itself during a heatwave. His own favourite among his novels, *Under the Greenwood Tree*, a gentle comedy, is set out in the four seasons.

But it is Gilbert White and his modern successors, today's natural history writers and broadcasters, topographers, meteorologists and conservationists, who continue to train us to understand the England of all seasons. We now have a more comprehensive local view than ever before, with a full awareness of all that surrounds us. And it's easy to get about and experience what were until recently almost inaccessible scenes. More importantly, we have been made to care for England, as a very special and wonderful ecology, as it has never previously been cared for. It has sometimes been claimed that when the National Trust, for example, takes coastlines, gardens, forests, mountains, etc. into its keeping, this is just a kind of topographical set-aside, a saving of particularly beautiful areas by roping them off into museums. But whilst taking such places out of threat, as it were, the National Trust is also showing itself to be a great popular educator. Lessons are driven home when we visit its possessions. Land-wise, these are now so extensive as to suggest a protected little kingdom whose laws and common sense are now extending into England at large. When we see the Hope Woodlands in Derbyshire, for instance, we immediately decide to retain such woods as are left on our own home ground. When we walk the huge commons near the New Forest we make up our minds not to let the old greens in our own neighbourhood perish under tarmac and 'leisure facilities'. What we recognize in such 'saved' corners and heights is not only what is becoming sadly absent elsewhere, but also an instruction on how to prevent loss of species, of quiet – the view itself – where we live. Such rescued scenes turn us into teachers, proselytes and defenders of an environment which all too easily these days can be mutilated.

At home we are constant watchers of the same view under a great range of seasonal influences. Few local scenes pall; on the contrary, familiarity seems to make them more intriguing. No hill or tree is the same for long. The daily sky puts the land through a whole sequence of illumination. Travelling, we are endlessly astonished at regional variety. The grand scene-shifts are the seasons. They alter everything. At their most extreme they can turn England into a succession of different countries and briefly transform the regional character of its inhabitants. But usually they offer a vision of landscape and architecture under passing conditions. We are really more affected by the brevity of spring and the length of winter than by the slipping away of an entire year.

Looking around has the effect of checking or stabilizing time. Very few acres of England, its hilltops excepted, have remained untouched by human hand over the millennia, yet, strangely and excitingly, it is the drifting nature of the seasons which confirms their permanence. Suffolk villagers would tell those who wished to get to know them that 'You will have to winter us and summer us', and this is what the explorer of England itself has to do. Accept that it is a country of all seasons. The use of landscape for refreshment and healing has long been known – the famous 'change of scene'. Landscape photography has become one of the most alluring parts of the traveller's tale and it always tells the seasons. It urges us to see Cumbria in February or to raise our eyes to different horizons, or to study the hedgerows and the ploughing. Most of all it proves how profoundly involved we are in an especially lovely scenery and how unthinkable it would be to have to live without it.

SPRING

SPANNING THE months from the vernal equinox to the summer solstice, the English spring combines all seasons. It is a succession of awakenings and surgings forward, of temperatures, of revelations. Neither man nor plant has ever been able to keep up with it. Until recently, it was not so much the stimulus of attempting to keep pace with its weather changes and moods which got both ourselves and the rest of creation going, as the perceptible flight from darkness. There was much dying in winter. To get through it was the thing. Days drawing out meant life drawing out. In Chaucer's magical poem *The Flower and the Leaf* all the knights and ladies emerge from their smoky winter halls to dance on the fresh grass and to do honour to – a daisy. Our first action in such a scene is to mow it. This spring I saw ten geese seated on a daisy-bank above a moat which was screened by blackthorn, and the triple whiteness of birds and flowers and clouds, I realized, was as special to spring as its verdancy. On an April day in 1870, Gerard Manley Hopkins saw the meadows 'deep green lighted underneath with white daisies'. In the north the daisy was always *the* flower of the spring. In my own Suffolk, though unrecognized before John Constable, it was the whiteness, not the greenness, which made the landscape live. It made his contemporaries laugh when he included it. His 'snow', it was called. But it was his accurate account of the spring.

So spring arrives before winter is out, and summer overtakes it long before mid-June, and it is a thin greening and a voluptuous opulence, and no one thing two days in a run. In February I do my staring at the bare earth walks. The farmland and the heaths are littered with shells, bones, flints and the minutiae of human existence. April will draw a veil over them. And it is a change to look up from a ground-fixed ramble to note solitary trees or the hard line of the horizon. England is full of lone features, natural and artificial, which have often been part of the symbolism of some local community for centuries, and the photograph has a way of extending their mystery. They stand out, naked and uncompromising during the early spring: oaks, tumuli, the sudden turn of an ancient path, an immense hawthorn like that which, as children, we learned to call the Satan Tree, although nobody told us why. Spring, when little can be hid, is a good time to take stock of the harshness of things. Spring, when May is here, is one bright spontaneous celebration, when it should be the feast of cow-parsley, for from now to June it will transform the road and rail networks and, given the chance, provide the perfect foil to Gothic architecture and turn churchyards and orchards into bridal acres.

Spring, early or late, freezing or burning, is for visiting the heaths and

Challock woods (previous page) to the north of Ashford in Kent photographed in the early spring.

wetlands. Never before have they been so treasured and understood. Rather the reverse; there used to be much speculation about the kind of people who could endure such spaces and levels, and who knew how to manage them. Evidence of this management becomes clear and accessible after the winter floods, and when one can explore Romney Marsh, Blakeney Point, Bodmin Moor or my own favourite Dunwich Heath without the wind trying to cut one's head off. Suffolk is edged with a wide band of sandlings which has its own rare botany, its own enchanting birdsong. Here, and on the Norfolk coast, one can actually smell the approach of spring, as Canadians or Russians smell it, far off but on the way.

In late spring there is no place like Cornwall, where the lane and field drystone 'hedges' are turned into hanging gardens, and the rills hurry along under hart's tongue and bracken. After Easter there is a grand uncovering of yachts, accommodation and programmes for the months ahead. More hauntingly, there is leading forth from his winter darkness the Padstow 'Oss, the most unlikely Persephone figure imaginable, and yet the only truly convincing remnant of England's pre-Christian spring rites. Like the dragonfly or, more aptly, the may-fly, the 'Oss's taste of the sunshine is brief and I have seen huge Cornish fishermen near to tears when he has to return to darkness. But the spring itself tears ahead like an ungovernable child, and there are the long walks which have become traditional, strenuous hikes across Pentire in misty rain, or along the Valency Valley, every step of which is part of Thomas Hardy's loving requiem for his courtship, or, going south, to Zennor. Cornwall's is an Atlantic spring. During May, although all are busying themselves for the rush to come, the richness of the flora seems only to emphasize the granite which forms the entire peninsula, and its oceanic setting, and it makes one feel frail and temporary – yet exhilarated.

Whenever I look down on as much Cornwall as I can hold in one great glance, from the Cheesewring, say, on Bodmin Moor, or from above the gardens on St Michael's Mount, Louis Aragon puts words into my mouth.

> O month of flowerings, month of metamorphoses, May without cloud
> and June that was stabbed, I shall never forget the lilac and the roses,
> nor those whom the spring has kept in its folds.

At home in the Stour Valley I observe the silence of the farms where, were it not for the wind, one could hear a pin drop. Neither farmer nor farm worker is seen for weeks on end. What do they do in the spring? In all the old rural calendars there were specific spring tasks, particularly spring carryings-on. But now only growth.

Spring flowers in the grounds of Leeds Castle in Kent.

The banks of a small stream in Airedale near Skipton, Yorkshire.
A late snowfall (overleaf) covers the gorse bloom on Exmoor
near Simonsbath in Somerset.

*Badgworthy Water (above top) in Exmoor near Oare in Somerset,
the setting for RD Blackmore's* Lorna Doone. *(Below) An early morning view in the
late spring of Dovedale in Derbyshire. (Opposite) An afternoon in the late spring
on the banks of Buttermere in Cumbria. (Overleaf) The North Downs in the late spring
close to the Pilgrims Way near Wrotham in Kent.*

*The first signs of spring in the Trough of Bowland
near Whitewell in Lancashire.*

*Countisbury Common near Lynmouth in North Devon photographed
at the end of April. (Overleaf) A freshly cut meadow photographed just before
sunset in the hills above Dovedale in Derbyshire.*

*A*n *early morning view (left) of the River Duddon near Ulpha in Dunnerdale,
Cumbria, photographed in April. (Above top) Hawthorn in full flower on the hills
above the River Wye near Bakewell in Derbyshire. (Below) Silver Birch budding
in the late spring on the shores of Buttermere in Cumbria. (Overleaf) Spring frost
melting in the early morning sunlight in Dunnerdale, Cumbria.*

*B*uttercups growing under a dry stone wall in Derbyshire.

Saxifrage blooming on a dry stone wall in Cumbria. (Overleaf) A brooding storm in the hills to the north of Coniston Water in Cumbria.

A dusting of snow at the beginning of May in the Brendon Hills near Wheddon Cross in Somerset.

Cow parsley growing beside a country lane near Crackington in Cornwall.
(Overleaf) Early morning spring sunshine in Borrowdale, Cumbria.

Hedgerow honeysuckle (left) in a Devon lane. (Above top) Early blooms in a country cottage garden near Tideswell in Derbyshire. (Below) Sissinghurst Garden in Kent photographed in the early spring. (Overleaf) Evening light in the early spring on Brendon Common in North Devon.

A cider-apple orchard in full blossom near Leominster, Hereford & Worcester.

An early crop of rape seed in full flower near the village of Duntisbourne Leer in Gloucestershire.

SUMMER

SUMMER'S START is confusing. No sooner does it begin than it is 'mid'. What happens is that the actual summer solstice on 21 June, when the sun reaches its zenith, is hotly followed by a feast which may have its origins in fiery attempts to placate those foul-weather powers which could ruin the coming harvest. This feast, Midsummer, on 24 June, was allocated to St John the Baptist who, as 'a burning and shining light', as Christ described him, deserved to be remembered at the peak of the year. His flower is St John's Wort (*Hypericum perforatum*), that flaming sun plant which, for our ancestors, was, leaf and bloom, an all-purpose remedy for sickness, body and soul. Summer sings, and the opening lines of St John's vesper hymn give us the names of the notes of the scale. The hymn asks 'that your servants may sing full-throatedly the marvels of your works, purify the guilt of their polluted lips, blessed John' – *Ut* queant laxis *re*sonare *fi*bris/*Mi*ra gestorum *fa*muli tuorum/*So*ve polluti *la*bii reatum/Sancte Johannes. The Italians changed *Ut* to *Do*. Thus we have Do, Re, Me, Fa, So, La . . .

Because of set-aside, the new agricultural policy of taking land out of corn and sowing it with grass, the hay harvest has returned with noticeable effect in the eastern counties. The old tangy sweetness of mown pastures fills the air. Except that these hayfields have never been grazed – it is not allowed. Early summer grasses are a delight but remain little understood or regarded. Country children of my generation sank into them. Just a few of them became as familiar and identifiable as trees or flowers, grasses such as the perennial Quaking-grass which occupied the same habitat for generations of human existence and which we picked to go with Moon Daisies, and Rye-grass from which to tell our Tinker-Tailor-Soldier-Sailor futures. The grassy hills and downs, their surfaces turned into green seas by summer winds, should be a matter of contemplation, like cloud-watching. In our age, the only really *seen* grass is the lawn. During summer the fine lawns of great houses, Cliveden, Polesden Lacey, Upton, Nostell Priory, and of the Oxford and Cambridge colleges evoke as much respect as fine art. Grass is said to symbolize our impermanence, but England's summer grasses, in their endlessly lovely renewal, would seem to refute this. August for the people, said W. H. Auden, but Midsummer for their matchless land of grass. Gilbert White, looking at the Selborne grass on a summer's day in 1778, wrote,

> But of all sorts of vegetation the grasses seem to be the most neglected; neither the farmer nor the grazier seems to distinguish the annual from the perennial, the hardy from the tender . . . The botanist that could improve the sward of a district where he lived would be an useful

*L*ate August on the moors (*previous page*) *above the village of Grinton in Swaledale, Yorkshire.*

member of society; to raise a thick turf on a naked soil would be worth volumes of systematic knowledge . . .

It is grass which holds the English landscape together: the watery grasses of Wicken Fen which grow alongside the sedge and reed, and which in summer can have that strange dryness peculiar to marsh plants; the grassy lanes among the Quantocks where during the 1790s three young friends, Coleridge and William and Dorothy Wordsworth, walked and wrote, composing on the hoof, as it were; and the silky grass of the Malvern Hills and Wenlock Edge.

Late summer is for the harvest and for the fading of birdsong. White found August to be the 'most mute month'. The harvest too is now so fast and quiet – just the drone of combines – that its total absence of village voices would have bewildered our grandparents. But the pale gold stubble remains, and the huge views, and even the aftermath, that interesting low growth of weeds which appears between the cutting and the ploughing. The camera has re-taught the lessons of the arable land. It draws our gaze to the yearly wonder of the crops and makes us recognize them as a beautiful necessary achievement. And when the fields are cleared it shows us what we would not normally see, the work-marks of history.

Summer is for leisure, for going about, for exploring and looking, for being pilgrims or plain Nosy Parkers. England is on display, its intricate, varied culture, its ever-changing regions, its gardens at their most sumptuous, and its superb architecture, beginning with Avebury Ring. It is the young who are drawn to the oldest places and who travel to discover the truth of myths. In summer they journey to the megalithic sun temples or to Glastonbury, King Arthur's isle of apples, finding their way by ley-lines. There is nothing like a heatwave to bring out their provocative indolence. They are a heliotropic or sun-turning race, as much a feature of the summer as the wild roses, but where do they go when the sun goes? The rest of us are lured from event to event, for the essence of summery England, it would appear, is the Event, the tour, the flower-show, the concerts in gardens and cathedrals, the sports, the rallies. But for many, like myself, summer is the time for perfecting the art of going nowhere, for simply being, for looking into the shimmering distance, for finding the old paths, for listening to the barley rustling, for appreciating the shade, for staring at darting fish in exquisite rivers such as the Test, for picking soft fruit and for reading out of doors. For, all too soon, as Kipling said, 'your English summer's done'.

*The Medway valley (above) in July near Penshurst in Kent.
(Opposite) A woodland walk near the village of Stourton in Wiltshire.
(Overleaf) Looking towards the North Downs from Seal Chart
near Sevenoaks in Kent.*

*Evening summer sunlight on Dartmoor, South Devon,
near the village of Poundsgate.*

A late summer evening (above) at Bell Tor on Dartmoor, South Devon.
(Overleaf) The patterns created by August stubble burning on the Marlborough Downs
near the village of Aldbourne in Wiltshire.

High summer (left) in the valley of the Test near the village of Longparish in Hampshire. (Above top) A hot August day in the wheatfields in the Rodings near Great Dunmow in Essex. (Below) Foxgloves at the edge of a copse on the North Downs near Kemsing in Kent. (Overleaf) A field of flax on a hillside above the Darent valley near Shoreham in Kent.

A freshly-cut hayfield left to dry in the evening sunlight
near Cerne Abbas in Dorset.

An early morning mist (above) settles on the wheatfields beside the Pilgrims Way near Ightham in Kent. (Overleaf) Poppies and ripening wheat in the Darent valley, Kent.

Summer flowers in the gardens of Fitz House in the village of Teffont Magna, Wiltshire.

A summer garden (above top) on the banks of the River Arrow in the village of Eardisland, Hereford & Worcester. (Below) A rose-covered cottage in the village of Appledore in Kent. (Overleaf) Looking westwards towards Wales on an August evening from the Long Mynd near Church Stretton in Shropshire.

*E*vening sunlight in late June on the South Downs near the village
of East Harting in West Sussex.

*Sheep resting under a solitary tree on the hills above the valley
of the Dove in Derbyshire. (Overleaf) Summer sunlight and green meadows in
Farndale in the North York Moors.*

*A*ugust hay bales in the Vale of Evesham near Mickleton in Gloucestershire.

*A flood of poppies in a set-aside field in the Darent valley
near Shoreham, Kent. (Overleaf) Looking westwards across Cuckmere Haven, Sussex,
just before sunset on a June evening.*

A high summer's view towards the east from Win Green in Wiltshire.

Looking westwards on a late summer afternoon from Fontmell Down in Wiltshire.

AUTUMN

'IF AUTUMN comes, can winter be far behind?' Because there was such a fear of winter, an absolute dread of it, autumn, the season which signalled it, was piled with doom-laden epithets. 'Drear' was the chief word for it. But allowing for the city smogs induced by so much coal-burning until the 1950s, and admitting that at the December end the daylight shrinks and there are freezing nights, could a time of the year which abounds with so much colour and fruit, and indeed with regular bursts of warmth such as those mid-October days known as 'St Luke's little summer', ever have deserved the reputation ascribed to it by generations of poets? English autumns, stripped of false rhetoric, need to be seen afresh. To regard them, as people did, as the sad analogy of their own decline, and to say, 'the best is past and the worst awaits', is to close one's eyes to some of the most vital splendours of the English year. Season of thoughtfulness, certainly, but not of despair. Don't miss a day of it. John Keats in his *The Human Seasons*, says that it is the time 'to look'.

Naturalists chalk up the dates of arrivals and departures. Migrating birds gather for the flight to Africa, and we realize with a pang that they belong as much to Morocco as to Hampshire. Orderly summer gardens, given half a chance, become unruly October gardens crammed with fauvist hues and tangled creepers. The brief interlude between harvest and sowing has to be seized on for stubble-walking. There is no better shake-up of an over familiar view than to see it via a little journey across cut fields. There is the parish church as the peasants saw it in the Middle Ages; there, under one's feet, is the aftermath, the low second growth which will shortly be ploughed-in, a soft mat of weed between the sharp corn-stalks. There are plenty of butterflies, Brimstones, Peacocks, Red Admirals, Painted Ladies, Tortoise-shells, all attracted to Michaelmas Daisies, knapweed, and some to fallen fruit.

Orchards may not be what they were, but there are still a lot of them about. The wise autumn traveller will make a point of noting the whereabouts of old country-house, farm, cottage and suburban orchards, and orchards hiding behind tall walls in small towns. Ribston, Cox's Orange and Blenheim Orange Pippin apples; greengages, England's oldest cultivated plum (they discovered greengage stones in the *Mary Rose*), damsons, rare pears and, if one is lucky, ancient mulberry trees and a sprawling Portugal quince. It is a comfort to know that here and there all over the country the English in autumn are devouring their matchless fruit. The hedgerows too are laden, yet at the same time strangely ignored. By September they are impacted with bryony, goosegrass and immense nettles, but their fruits hang thick: blackberries, spindle, hazel-nuts, elderberries, sloes, bullace-plums, hips and

October sunlight (previous page) in the woods at Oldbury Hill near Ightham in Kent.

haws, and the seed-heads of numerous summer flowers. By December the hedges have thinned to screens of sticks through which can be glimpsed the winter wheat, but which still manage to provide a tolerable wind barrier.

The landscape itself follows a similar progression. Until mid-November it is opulent, bursting with colour, with summery achievements, then it begins to show its bones. The bare facts are at first disconcerting. How can so many leaves vanish or so many branches exist? The ground is covered with cobwebs. Rooks call from swaying colonies. Gilbert White, who liked to begin his parlour fires as soon as autumn began, was no stay-at-home when, for most people, weather became forbidding. He would walk out to admire the 'beautiful picturesque, partial fogs along the vales, representing rivers, islands and arms of the sea'. Walking becomes brisk after October. Footsteps ring out on frosty roads or are muted on their damp and filmy surface, or kick their way pleasantly, like a child, through papery leaves and beech-mast. It is an excellent time to see what the inhabitants of this island used to see before Christ – the Oxfordshire hill-forts, Ditchling Beacon, the first tracks. For these ancient places now possess both their own special end-of-year clarity, and misty edges which test the imagination.

Autumn is for the harvest moon and the hunter's moon, for hornets crashing among the vines, for wood-smoke, for village lights, for Traveller's Joy, for having the beach to yourself, for clearing up the summer residue, for re-reading favourite books or starting to write a new one, for the sweet smell of vegetable dissolution, for watching homing birds, for making jam and wine, for being nicely tired. It is time to remember to see Cotehele, Canons Ashby, Blickling and Cartmel before their gates swing to for the winter. Also to remember that mountains, commons, woods, rivers and the old roads which lead to them do not close down for the season, but all through these golden, soaking, blowing days, left to themselves, are once more embarked upon the everlasting circle of regeneration.

*A*utumnal berries on the North Downs near the village of Otford in Kent.

Beech woods (above) in Knole Park near Sevenoaks in Kent.
(Overleaf) Late autumn at Tarn Hows near Hawkshead in Cumbria.

*Mature trees in autumn colours (left) at Burnham Beeches near Slough in Berkshire.
(Above) Oldbury Hill woods near Ightham in Kent.
(Overleaf) Evening sunlight in late October on the North Downs
near Wrotham in Kent.*

*F*ishpond woods (above) near Ightham in Kent photographed in the late autumn.
(Opposite) Evening sunlight at the end of autumn near the village of Heaverham in Kent.
(Overleaf) The last of the autumn colour on the hillsides around Tarn Hows
near Hawkshead in Cumbria.

*A bough of russet leaves (left) at Burnham Beeches in Berkshire.
(Above) Autumn leaves and berries colour the bushes
lining the Pilgrims Way near Otford in Kent.
(Overleaf) Looking eastwards in the late autumn at Gara Rock
near Start Point in South Devon.*

A Rowan tree in full fruit on Arden Great Moor near Hawnby in North Yorkshire.

*Late autumn in the countryside of the South Hams near Newton Abbot, Devon.
(Overleaf) Early autumn sunshine in the Cleveland Hills
near Osmotherley, North Yorkshire.*

A crisp autumn day close to the Ridgeway on the Lambourn Downs in Berkshire.

*E*mpty *October hopfields in the Darent valley near Shoreham in Kent.*
(Overleaf) Newly-planted crops emerging in late autumn near Kingsbridge, South Devon.

Autumn leaves on an ancient tree in Knole Park near Sevenoaks, Kent.

*E*arly autumn colours in the bracken at Oldbury Hill woods
near Ightham in Kent. (Overleaf) Red bracken colours the hillsides
in the late autumn in Dunnerdale, Cumbria.

*E*arly autumn in the tiny valley of Westerdale near
Castleton in the North York Moors.

A meadow below the North Downs near the village of Heaverham in Kent.

WINTER

G EOGRAPHICALLY, the English winter is mapped out by degrees of intensity. Usually, it is at its loveliest when at its hardest, on the great moors and among the peaks. Moorland under snow, headlands in cutting winds, any garden seized by hoar-frost, a river turned to thick ice, any wild or tamed landscape being given a hard (and beautiful) time by a plunge in the temperature, tends to leave us in shock. It is because at the close of the second millennium we have persuaded ourselves that we have got the measure of the cold. But we haven't and we never will. All the same, when that 'snow on snow' of the carol refuses every now and then to confine itself to the bitter old days, we are surprised and made helpless. We, the citizens of the thermalized age, cannot keep out the cold. We have paid a small fortune to bar it from our existence – yet, in a real winter, the cold comes in. It certainly enters some parts of the countryside with a despotism which takes our breath away, with an unbearable glory and with a power which subdues rocks, escarpments and the very sky itself. Going anywhere near the Pennines, Dartmoor or Helvellyn during a big freeze would be mad and anti-social – but what sights! And what ultimate knowledge of winter in England. But perhaps there is a climatic justice that in deepest winter most of the well-trodden heights along the Pennine Way, in Derbyshire, Rough Tor and Brown Willie on the Cornish moors, and the Langdale Pikes in the Lake District, revert to their natural isolation.

For all the convention and the wishfulness of seeing it thus, snow is not the main characteristic of an English winter. Severity is patchy, and what we have are long stretches of cool greyness whipped up now and then by gales, or briefly dispersed by sunshine. The soft colouring is often misunderstood and labelled dull, but it is frequently what the English abroad miss most. It is in fact a perfect basic shade for the scenery of these islands, a living grey which in February, the most accused 'grey' month, backs up a great range of wintry colour: terra-cotta, crimson, ochre, streaky yellow and the purest azure when the light pours in. The water-colour, England's native and unrivalled art-form, owes more to winter than to any other season.

Old lost landscapes are briefly recovered in winter. The pattern made by the first ploughs and the first travellers reappears. The season becomes a clearing-house for the ephemeral, the non-essential and the perishable, all of which fade from sight, leaving the basic structure of the countryside exposed. The scenery becomes an open book with tell-tale evidence to show that each page has been gone over several times. In a few months the evidence will be obliterated by plants and all the ancient markings will vanish under corn, trees and flowers. But during January the magnitude of this annual growth

A winter's day at dusk (previous page) in Fishpond woods near the village of Ightham in Kent.

can hardly be conceived. The seasons are difficult to remember accurately out of season. Winter is the time for reversing our opportunism, and instead of – or as well as – grabbing all we can of summer, we should lay hands on what winter can offer: a glimpse of Iron Age and Celtic England, starkly beautiful forests, icily creaking marshes, and most particularly the sea shore clear for miles beneath a sun without heat.

Winter beaches provide tremendous elemental experiences. Whether calm or wild, they are the place for visionaries, or simply for clearing one's head. Whilst the relics of summer are still being cast around by the waves, rubbish which can neither dissolve nor escape, it is the wailing birds who are in full possession of the coast now. They scream and float in great numbers from the northern preserves to the vast cliffs beyond Boscastle, creating around England a white, complaining universe in motion. A human being is never more out of his own element than when he is struggling along West Country sands and rocks, or Suffolk's shingle ridge on a stormy winter's day, and he knows it. Huge distances can be clearly seen one minute and blocked off the next. The air is piercingly fresh and yet at the same time reeking of salt and fish. Alarmingly near, great holes in the sea itself set up a thunder and one feels exhilarated but unsafe.

The interior, by contrast, can be motionless, more still than at any other time of the year. Away from the main traffic one can listen to the winter quiet of the old settlements, and from heights such as Cissbury Ring, Boars Hill or the parapet of any country town or village church, pick out an extraordinary number of landscape features which, unless frozen in the photographer's frame, one would have assumed could now only be found in Tudor plays or Jane Austen's novels. Artists have always been attracted to a winter-locked view in which everything is alive, although nothing moves. Others find such days sulky and lowering. They say they can't keep warm and that the sun hasn't shone since October, and ask who would live in England in winter if they didn't have to? It is useless to preach the pleasures and compensations of winter. Few have a good word for it. Yet there is no time like it for tramping about the counties as though on a relief map where every feature is plain to see. There is the archaeology of the fallow fields, the rookeries, the failing light in the afternoon garden, the limit to what can be done, although none to what can be felt and seen – in spite of mists.

Evening sunlight in late January on the North York Moors near Osmotherley.

Looking westwards from the top of Fontmell Down in Wiltshire on a late February afternoon. (Overleaf) December snow coats the trees on the shores of Lake Windermere near Ambleside in Cumbria.

A February hoar frost settles in the Darent valley near Shoreham in Kent.

A January sunset colours the sky over fields near Beckley in East Sussex. (Overleaf) Looking westwards over Redmire Moor on the heights between Wensleydale and Swaledale, Yorkshire.

*A January evening (left) in the meadows of the Medway valley
near Tonbridge in Kent. (Above top) Frosted leaves melting
in the early morning sunlight in Fishpond woods
near Ightham in Kent. (Below) A layer of ice covers
the fallen leaves in Fishpond woods. (Overleaf)
Looking westwards towards Simons Fell near
Horton-in-Ribblesdale, Yorkshire.*

A heavy December snowfall at Matterdale End near Ullswater in Cumbria.

*A winter mist in the early morning on Seal Chart near Sevenoaks in Kent.
(Overleaf) Looking east just before sunset on a December evening from
Hard Knott Pass in Cumbria.*

A bright crisp February afternoon (left) on Winchelsea beach in East Sussex.
(Above) on Redmire Moor above Wensleydale photographed on a late January afternoon.
(Overleaf) The first snows of winter cover the floor of the valley
near Troutbeck in Cumbria.

*Early catkins showing in January on the Hambleton Hills near Hawnby
in the North York Moors.*

A cold January day on the Isle of Oxney near the village of Wittersham in Kent. (Overleaf) A dusting of snow covers the bracken on Wythburn Fells near Grasmere in Cumbria.

*An early December morning in the Troutbeck valley near Windermere in Cumbria.
(Opposite) A newly-ploughed field on a late winter's afternoon in
the Wylye valley, Wiltshire. (Overleaf) Looking east in the evening sunlight towards
Golden Cap near Chideock in Dorset.*